PEN & BRUSH
LETTERING

PEN & BRUSH LETTERING

A BOOK OF ALPHABETS

STUDIO
VISTA

Studio Vista
a Cassell imprint

Wellington House, 125 Strand
London, WC2R 0BB

First published in this edition 1993
Reprinted 1994
Reprinted 1995
Reprinted 1997

British Library Cataloguing in Publication Data
A catalogue record for this book is available from the British Library

ISBN 0 289 80099 4

This book is a combined edition of
Pen & Brush Lettering & Alphabets
(first published 1929, sixteenth edition 1986, reprinted twice 1991)
and *Script Lettering*
(first published 1956, second edition 1964, reprinted 1991)

Distributed in the United States
by Sterling Publishing Co. Inc,
387 Park Avenue South, New York, NY 10016

Printed and bound in Great Britain
at The Bath Press, Bath

Contents

Introduction

The lettering we use today has been handed down from early times. Our present main upright alphabet, whatever variety or 'face' it may have, was derived from the Romans and is still known as 'Roman'. It has serenity, repose, and simplicity; and above all a clarity which makes it one of the greatest symbols of civilization. The classical proportions of the Roman alphabet have served for more than 2,000 years as a base from which lettering styles can be developed to serve particular purposes, and today the number of alphabets and styles in use is almost beyond number.

In these times of sophisticated graphics and persistent marketing techniques so much depends on lettering to convey meaning and emotion. The choice and use of lettering has become an art, calling at all times for a skill and originality based on an understanding of what lettering is and how it works. Lettering can shout, or it can whisper; it can be crude or refined, urgent or restrained, blatant or amost invisible. Each alphabet expresses something different, and carries a message beyond the simple words into which it is arranged.

The following pages contain a selection of alphabets to act as a reference to the student, designer and commercial artist. The alphabets are divided broadly into sections: Serif, Italic, Sans Serif, Shadow, Script, Old English, Numerals, and unusual styles. Where samples of type are shown they are mostly selected from the Monotype range. The alphabets have been chosen to cover a wide range of possible uses; but how they are used is, of course, up to the artist or designer. As a general rule it is usually best to avoid numerous styles of lettering on one design, which can lead to a loss of legibility and consequent confusion, but experiment and practice will soon show even the beginner how to find the right effect with a suitable lettering. From the alphabets in this book, necessarily limited but representative of the many in use today, the artist will find sufficient material to exercise, and then further develop, his or her creative imagination.

ABCDEFGI
HJKLMNO
PQRSTUV
WXYZ

Perpetua Light Titling has the matchless proportions of
the classical Roman letter.

abcdefghij
klmnopqr
stuvwxyz

Perpetua Roman lower case.

ABCDEFGH
IJKLMNOP
QRSTUVW
XYZ

abcdefghijklm
nopqrstuvwxyz

Bodoni A much used modern style Roman in which strength is
combined with delicacy by means of contrasting heavy descenders
and fine ascenders.

ABCDEFGH
IJKLMNOP
QRSTUVW
XYZ

abcdefghijk
lmnopqrstu
vwxyz

Ultra Bodoni This striking, heavy letter gives an
effect of weight and boldness.

ABCDEFGHIJ KLMNOPQR STUVWXYZ

abcdefghij klmnopqr stuvwxyz

Bembo One of the loveliest of all old-face designs.

ABCDEFGH
IJKLMNO
PQRSTUV
WXYZ

abcdefgh
ijklmnopq
rstuvwxyz

Times Bold A twentieth-century contribution to type design.

ABCDEFGHIJ
KLMNOPQRS
TUVWXYZ

abcdefghij
klmnopqrs
tuvwxyz

Slim Black A condensed letter of distinction.

ABCDEFGHJ

KLMNOPQR

STUVWXYZ

abcdefghijkln
mopqrstuw
vxyz

Monarch A pen-lettered alphabet combining strength with dignity.
Its characteristic serifs can best be put in finally with the brush.

ABCDEFGHIJ
KLMNOPQR
STUVWXYZ

abcdefghijklm
nopqrstuvwxyz

Rockwell An even-thickness letter with slab serifs.

ABCDEFGHIJ
KLMNOPQR
STVUWXYZ

abcdefghijklm
nopqrstuvwxyz

Perpetua The italic form of the alphabet on page 7. Note the slight
modification in the proportion of letters, and the elliptical curves.

ABCDE
FGHIJK
LMNOP
QRSTU
VWXYZ

A single-stroke broad-nib alphabet of classical proportions. A good
example of fine penmanship of a style used in formal work.

a b c d e f
g h i j k l
m n o p q
r s t u v
w x y z

ABCDEFGH
IJKLMNOP
QRSTUVW
XYZ

abcdefghijklmn
opqrstuvwxyz

Gill Bold Sans Serif Italic

ABCDEFG
HIJKLMN
OPQRSTU
VWXYZ

abcdefghij
klmnopqr
stuvwxyz

Times Bold Italic The italic version of the alphabet shown on
page 11.

ABCDEFGHIJ
KLMNOPQRS
TUVWXYZ&

abcdefghijklmno
pqrstuvwxyz

1234567890

Goudy Bold Italic An attractive, legible letter, which has more
strength than most of the italic faces.

A B C D E F G

H I J K L M N

O P Q R S T U

V W X Y Z

a b c d e f g h i j k l m

n o p q r s t u v w x y z

1 2 3 4 5 6 7 8 9 0

A single-stroke pen alphabet. This is particularly suitable for rapid
showcard and price ticket work, as its very essence is simplicity.
For this page a Myers No. 1 broad nib was used.

ABCDEFG HIJKLMN OPQRSTU VWXYZ

abcdefghi jklmnopqr stuvwxyz

1234567890

A slightly expanded italic sans-serif letter, based on FTF's 'Washington' design. For best effect it should be used sparingly, and with plenty of white space.

ABCDEF GHIJKL MNOPQ RSTUVW XYZ

abcdefghijklmn
opqrstuvwxyz

Gill Sans Titling A legible, pleasant and very readable face. Suitable for headings where copy is short, but if used to any great extent the effect is monotonous. Gill Sans lower case is shown in the frame.

ABCDE
FGHIJK
LMNOP
QRSTU
VWXYZ

Gill Sans Bold Titling gives weight.

ABCDEFG
HIJKLMN
OPQRSTU
VWXYZ

abcdefghij
klmnopqr
stuvwxyz

Gill Sans Extra Bold gives emphasis and strength.

ABCDEFGHIJKL
MNOPQRSTU
VWXYZ&

abcdefghijklmn
opqrstuvwxyz

1234567890

Futura Light A notable contribution to the sans serif series and
especially useful where delicacy of effect is desired.

ABCDEFG
HIJKLMN
OPQRST
UVWXYZ

abcdefghijklmn
opqrstuvwxyz

Albertus has a distinct character of its own and in its conformation
is not unlike Gill.

ABCDEFGHIJK

LMNOPQRST

UVWXYZ&

Gothic Condensed A letter of a very striking design in the sans serif class. As with all condensed types, this can be used where economy of space is necessary.

abcdefghijkl mnopqrstuv wxyz

1234567890

ABCDEFG
HIJKLMN
OPQRSTU
VWXYZ

Elongated Roman Shaded

ABCDEFG
HIJKLMN
OPQRSTU
VWXYZ

Sans Serif Shaded An elongated style with legibility and
distinction.

ABCDE
FGHIJK
LMNOPV
QRSTU
WXYZ
1234567
890

Gill Shadow The shadow effect here gives a sense of considerable depth.

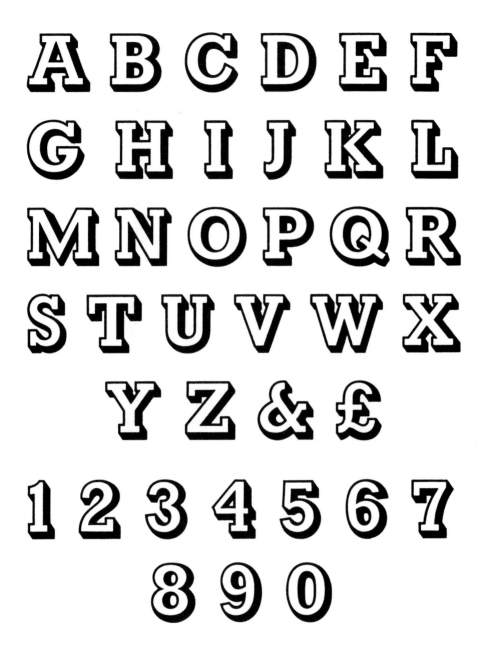

Rockwell Shadow A sturdy letter that looks effective
in either one or two colours.

A B C D E
F G H I J
K L M N
O P Q R
S T U V
W X Y Z

A Roman letter with an unusual shading effect.

ABCDEFG
HIJKLMN
OPQRSTU
VWXYZ&

abcdefghijklmnopqrstu
vwxyz

1234567890

Bernhard Cursive Bold There is much grace in the form of this
modern script.

A B C D E
F G H I J
K L M N O
P Q R S T
U V V W
W X Y Z

abcdefghijklmn
oppqrstuvwxy

Pen Script, as this style is known, is one of the oldest forms of script
and remains in everyday use.

ABCDEFI
GHIKLMN
OPQRSTU
* VWXYZ *

abcdefghijklmno
pqrst·uvwxyz

Old English Script

ABCDEFJ
KLMNQR
STUVWX
YZ
abcd efgh
ijklmnopqrst
uwxyz

Gothic Script

ABCDEFGHJK
LMNOPQRS
TUVWXYZ

abcdefghijkln
mopqrstuw
vxyz

abcdefgihjklmno
pqrstuvwxyz

ABCDEFGHIJ
KLMNOPT
QRSUVX
+WYZ+

This script shows a celtic influence in the capital.

ABCDEFG
HIJKLMNO
PQRSTUW
VXYZ

abcde
fghijklmnopq
rstuvwxyz **

A gothic script with elongated and condensed capitals.

abcdefghijklmn
opqrstuvwxyz··

ABCDEFG
HIJKLMN
OPQRSTU
VWXYZ·

A free script with square forms.

ABCDEFG
HIJKLMNOP
QRSTUVWXY
Z

abcd efgh
ijklmnopqrstuv
wxyz

An elegant italic script.

abcdefghijklmn
opqrstuvwxyz

ABCDEFG
HIJKLMN
OPQRSTU
VWXYZ

This formal script has upright characters based on old style text.

abcdefghijklmnopq
rstuvwxyz

ABCDEFGHI
JKLMNOPQR
STUVW
XYZ

These sharp, narrow forms must be used
carefully to preserve legibility.

An open, flamboyant script, to be used sparingly, but to great effect.

ABCDEFG
HIJKLMNO
PQRSTUV
WXYZ

abcdefghijkl
mnopqrst
uvwxyz

Here, the flourishes are particularly strong in the capitals.

abcdefghijklm
nopqrstuvwxz

ABCDEF
GHIJKLM
NOPRSTU
VWXYZ

This script with rather more elegant, if less legible, flourishes in the
capitals is moving toward copperplate.

abcdefghijklmn
·opqrstuvwxyz·

ABCDEFGI
HIJKLMNO
PQRSTUVW
XYZ

A formal script showing copperplate influence.

A B C D E F G
H I J K L M
N O P Q R S T
U V W X Y Z

a b c d e f g h i j k l m n o
p q r s t u v w x y z

A heavy form of copperplate.

ABCDEFGI
HIJKLMNO
PQRSTUW
VXab hiYZ

cdefg
jklmnopqrstuvwxyz

A copperplate with flourishes in the capitals.

A copperplate with considerable flourishes in the capitals.

ABCDEFG
HIJKLMN
OPQRSTUV
WXYZ

abcdefghijklmn
opqrstuvwxyz

A heavy script in copperplate style.

ABCDEFG
HIJKLMN
QPRSTUV
WXYZ

abcdefgh
ijklmnopqrstuvw
xyz

A heavy, formal script with a strong copperplate influence.

ABCDEFGH
IJKLMNOP
QRSTUVWX
YZ

abcde   fghijk
lmnopqrstuvwxyz

Less heavy, more open, noticeably flourished
and showing some copperplate influence.

ABCD
EFGHIJ
JKLMN
OPQRS
TUVWX
YZ
abcdefghijkl
mnopqrstuvwxyz

A popular brush script.

ABCDEFGH
IJKLMNOPQ
RSTUVWXYZ

abcdefghijklm
nopqrstuvwxz

A light informal script with round upright characters.

An extra light informal brush script.

ABCDEFGH
JKLMMNO
PQRSTUVW
XYZ

abcdefghijklmnopq
rstuvwxyz

This brush script has rounded forms.

abcdefghijklmn
opqrstuvwxyz *

ABCDEFGH
IJKLMNOPQ
RSTUVWYZ

A free-flowing brush script.

ABCDEFGHIJK
CMNOPQRS
TUVWXYZ

abcdefghijklmnopq
rstuvwxyz

Equally free-flowing, but bolder and stronger.

abcdefghijklmn
opqrstuvwxyz

ABCDEFG
HIJKLMNO
PQRSTUW
VXYZ

Brush letters with strong, clear forms.

ABCDEFGH
IJKLMNOP
QRSTUVWXY
Z

abcdefg hijklmn
opqrstuvwxyz

A light, informal pen script in a very free style.

ABC
DEFGHIJKLMN
OPQRSTUVW
XYZ

abcdefghijklmnopr
stuvw   qxyz

This is a formal, upright script.

ABCDEF
GHIJKLM
NOPQRS
TUVWXYZ

abcdefghijklm
nopqrstuvwxz

The lower case is clear and formal here, noticeably more legible than
the capitals.

ABCD
EFGHIJK
LMNOPQ
RSTUVWX
YZ

abcdefghijkl
mnopqrstuvwxyz

A square-formed script with flourished capitals.

abcdefghijk
lmnopqrstuvw
xyz
ABC DEF
GHIJKLMNO
PQRSTUVW
XYZ

Similar in character to 66, but more freely expressed.

ABCDEF
GHIJKLM
NOPQRST
UVWXYZ
abcdefghijkl
mnopqrstuvw
xyz

Informal characters with a squat lower case.

A A B C D E F F G G H H I
J K K L M M N N O P Q Q R
S S T U V W X Y Z 1234567890
abcdefghijklmnopqrstuvwxyz e h l r s t z

Graphic Script Bold Designed by Ernst Schneidler.
A nineteenth-century copperplate script.

A B C D E F G H I J K L M
N O P Q R S T U V W X Y Z
abcdefghijklmnopqrstuvwxyz

Kunstlerschreibschrift This script has the design of a copperplate
in a bold weight.

ABCDEFGHIJKLMN
OPQRSTUVWXYZ&
abcdefghijklmnopqrstuvwxyz

Dorchester Script A visitingcard script. A nearly upright type with curly capitals. The lower case has looped ascenders and long descenders.

ABCDEFGHIJKLMNO
PQRSTUVWXYZ
abcdefghijklmnopqrstuvwxyz
1234567890

Copperplate Bold A bold face of the English copperplate script.

ABCDEFGHIJKLMNOPQuRST
UVWXYZ

abcdefghijklmnopqrstuvwxyz   1234567890

ABCDEFGHIJKLMNOPQuRST
UVWXYZ   abcdefghijklmnopqrstuvwxyz

Rondo The flourished capitals have some resemblance to those of
the traditional French Ronde, but not the lower case. The variation of
colour is small, ascenders and descenders are short and there are
no looped letters. The type has a slight inclincation.
There are two weights.

ABCDEFGHIJKLMNOPQRSTUVWXYZ&
1234567890$abcdefghijklmnopqrstuvwxyz
AAEFGHIKLMNTVW&fh

Thompson Quillscript A calligraphic script with slight inclination.

ABCDEFGHIJKLMNOPQuRS
TUVWXYZÇÆŒ
abcdefghijklmnopqrstuvwxyzçœœ
1234567890

Rondine A formal script of medium weight. The capitals are freely
drawn, and in the lower case the ascenders are tall and looped.

ABCDEFGHIJKLMNOPQ
RSTUVWXYZ abcdefghijklmnopqrstuvwxyz
1234567890

Sinfonia or Stradivarius An unusual script with flourished
capitals and a stiff lower case. There is considerable variation of
colour. Ascenders are tall and there are no serifs. The rigid
appearance is produced by the squaring of normally round letters.

ABCDEFGHIJKLMNOPQRSTUVWXYZ
abcdefghijklmnopqrstuvwxyz 1234567890

Graphik or Herald A bold, slightly inclined script following the style of other German bold display scripts.

ABCDEFGHIJKLMNOPQ
RSTUVWYZ
abcdefghijklmnopqrstuvwxyz

Mercurius A heavy brush script of very angular design.

ABCDEFTIGHIIKLMNOPQÜRSSchSTTh
UVWXYZ 1234567890

aäubcdeeienerentfffifffgghhchheitijkckkeit

Reporter An informal script of medium weight which is slightly shaded.

ABCDEFGHIJKLMNOPQRSTUVWXYZ
abcdefghijklmnopqrstuvwxyz
1234567890

Mistral An informal, true script.

ABCDEFGHIJKLMNOPQRSTUVWXYZ

abcdefghijklmnopqrstuvwxyz   Th   1234567890

Gillies Gothic or Flott A script monotone in colour with flowing capitals and a rigid lower case.

ABCDEFGHIJKLMNOPQRSTUVW

XYZ&$£1234567890

abcdefghijklmnopqrssttthuvwxyz

Reiner Black A strong brush script.   75

ABCDEFGHIJKLMNOPQRSTUV

abcdefghijklmnopqrstuvwxyz

1234567890

BCDEFGIKOUVWY

Holla A quill pen-drawn script of medium weight.

ABCDEFGHIJKLMNOP

QRSTUVWXYZ

abcdefghijklmnopqrstuvwxyz

Saltino An informal Latin script of heavy weight and considerable
variation of stress.

LMNOPQRSTUV3

mnopqrstuvwxyzœ

24680!

with much variation of stress and tall ascenders.

Sam
"Instructed of God"

Hebrew. 11:3

Through Faith we understand
that the worlds were framed by the
Word of God ...

Samuel ?
Steven.

ABCDEFGHIJKLMNOPQRSTU
VWXYZŒ
abcdefghijklmnopqrrsstuvwxyz:æ

Bolide A heavy informal script with uneven outlines.

ABCDEFGHIJKLMNO

abcdefghijklmnopqrstuvwxyz

1234567890

ABCDEFGHIJKLMNO

abcdefghijklmnopqrstuvwxyz

Discus A formal script with moderate variation of stress and slight inclination.

ABCDEFGHIJKLMNO

PQRSTUVWXYZ

abcdefghijklmnopqrstuvwxyz

Palomba A script of heavy weight with flourished capitals and an upright lower case. Ascenders are tall and the letters have a pen-drawn quality with little variation of colour.

ABCDEFGHIJKLMNOPQRSTUV
WXYZ& abcdefghijklmnopqrstuvwxyz 1234567890

ABCDEFGHIJKLMNOPQRST
UVWX abcdefghijklmnopqrstuvwxyz
12334567890

Murray Hill A light script with swash capitals and an informal,
condensed lower case. The letters are almost upright.

ABCDEFGHIJKLMNOPQRSTUVWXYZÇÆŒ
abcdefghijklmnopqrsstuvwxyzç œœ
1234567890

Fluidium A script in which the thin strokes are hair lines.

ABCDEFG
HIJKLMN
OPQRSTU
VWXYZ

abcdefghijklm
nopqrstuvwxyz

Trafton A one-stroke letter dependent for its beauty on the even
flow of the letters. A valuable time-saver and favourite for
hand-written price tickets and showcards.

A B C D E
F G H I J K
L M N O P
Q R S T U
V W X Y Z

This elegant yet legible style can be utilized for initials in many
styles of lettering, both upright and sloping, and for the body matter
in illuminated addresses, testimonials, etc.

ABCDEFG HIJKLMN OPQRSTU VWXYZ

abcdefghi
jklmnopqr
stuvwxyz

An alphabet resembling 'Signal'. Heavy condensed scripts produce
here and there areas of inarticulate darkness which reduce
legibility. These have to be eliminated by tricks, slight falsities to the
true rhythm of the style.

New Season's Displays The Scotchman

—Fastest Time Ever!

Old French Porcelain

A New Airline...

Yachting Club

Express When a jazz man's blue...

New World Exhibitions

Good Food News The largest range

A new Overseas Journal

United States Lines

Script lettering can speak with a variety of intonation – sometimes
elegant, or exciting; perhaps regal or racy.

Masculine

Script for Stylo

Parchment

Sophisticated

Ball-pointed

Pen application.

Moist *Feminine*

or dry —

or both

Texture

Very Informal *Textile*

Calligraphy

Brush application.

the DEGREE of and the Quality

exaggeration

Possible

in Advertising script

is determined by

the structure

Varieties of script showing its endless possibilities.

of the letters—
especially
of the first letters
AND
and by the Message
or words
of the
WORD
that must be
written

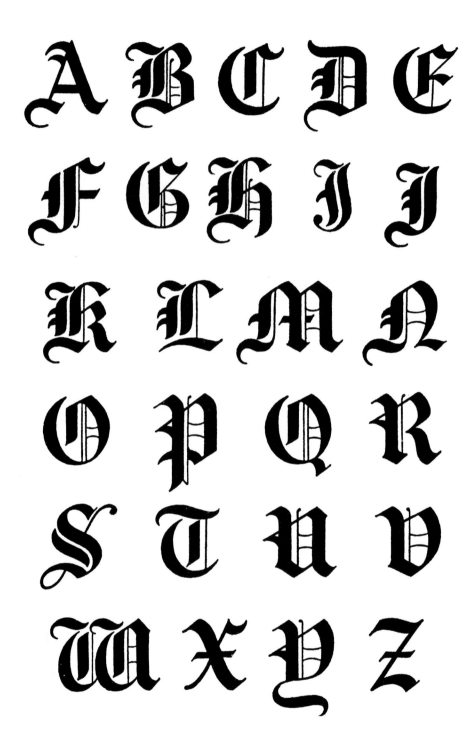

Old English This straight-sided angular Gothic letter was the original style used for the printed page. There are, of course, many different interpretations in present-day use, but the basic forms remain the same. Hair lines for embellishment should be avoided since they detract from legibility.

Old English Lower Case

1 2 3
4 5 6 7 8 9 0

Condensed Sans Serif

1 2 3
4 5 6 7 8 9 0

Gill Sans Bold Condensed

1 2 3
4 5 6 7 8 9 0

Trafton

1 2 3
4 5 6 7 8 9 0

Free and easy style for script lettering.

1 2 3
4 5 6 7 8 9 0

Perpetua

1 2 3
4 5 6 7 8 9 0

Gill Sans Medium Italic

ABCDEFGHIJKLM
NOPQRSTUVWXYZ
CENTURY
abcdefghijklm
nopqrstuvwxyz
123456789

Playbill This dates from the great days of the theatre poster and makes a heavy impact with slab-like serifs and the emphasis on horizontal strokes which is in contrast to almost every other letter-form. Still surprisingly popular, it is an effective display face.

A B C D E F G
H I J K L M N
O P Q R S T U
V W X Y Z

a b c d e f g h
i j k l m n o p q
r s t u v w x y z

1 2 3 4 5 6 7 8 9

Studio Based on the Amsterdam Type Foundry's design, this is a
modern one-stroke alphabet, especially suitable for showcard work.

ABCDEFGHIJ KLMNOPQRS TUVWXYZ&

abcdefghijklm nopqrstuvwxyz

1234567890

Metropolis A modern heavy letter, almost in the spirit of
Ultra Bodoni, but free in its style.

ABCDEFG
HIJKLMN
OPQRSTU
VWXYZ

abcdefghijk
lmnopqrstuv
wxyz

1234567890

An italic slab serif letter, based on Ludlow Karnak heavy italic
(by courtesy of Odhams Press). This style of heavy squat letter is much
favoured for exhibition signs and shop fascia board work.

ABCDE
FGHIJK
LMNOP
QRSTU
VWXYZ

Stencil Based on the actual form of letters stencilled on packing
cases, this face gives a note of the unusual.

ABCDEFGHI
JKLMNOPQR
STUVWXY & Z

abcdefghijklm
nopqrs_tuvwx
y and 3/

Modern Thick and Thin The letter height is twice as thick as the
average width.

ABCDEF
GHIJKLN
MOPQRS
TUVWXY
Z&
123456789

Adapted from the well-known printer's type 'Cooper Black'.
A speedy bold alphabet for poster and showcard work.

abcdefgh
ijklmnop
qrstuvwx
yz

The lower case of the alphabet opposite. The style combines
maximum boldness with clear-cut lines and complete legibility.

ABCDEF GHIJKL MNOPQ RSTUV WXYZ

Another modern thick and thin sans serif, which is extremely well designed, derived from Crous Vidal's 'Paris' typeface. This italic version has many possible variations and weights.

ABCDEF
GHIJKL
MNOPQ
RSTUVW
XYZ abcdefghijk
lmnopqrstuvwxyz !_?

Modern French for work requiring a light letter of simplicity and a
touch of exclusiveness.

ABCDEFGHIJ KLMNOPQRS TUVWXYZ

abcdefghijklm nopqrstuvwxyz

1234567890

An example of brush script lettering based on ATF's 'Dom Casual', designed by Peter Dom.

ABCDEF
GHIJKLM
NOPQRST
UVWXYZ

abcdefghij
klmnopqrst
uvwxyz&!?

Eastern An alphabet designed on Oriental characters, principally
the wedge in the crescent. There are obvious occasions for its use
and it is quickly written.

Christmas An example of how a seasonal atmosphere can be introduced into the letter.

Pen-written Capitals From *The Pen's Transcendency*, a Writing Book
by E. Cocker, 1660. Cocker was so emphatically the English writing-master
of his day as to have given rise to the phrase, 'According to Cocker'.

ABCD

IIKLM

RSTUV

EFGH

NOPQ

WPYZ

Modern Gothic Capitals Fanciful, but no violence to accepted
form. An alphabet in which it is permitted even to hide the meaning
so long as it is still there.

ABCDEFG
HIJKLMN
OPQRSTU
VWXYZ&
abcdefghijk
lmnopqrstu
vwxyz& ·§·
1234567890

Pen-written Alphabets and Numerals Percy J. Smith.

abcde
efghi
klmn
opqrs
stuvx

Stone Lettering From inscriptions at Osnabrück, Germany.
Halting between majuscule and miniscule forms. 1742-56.

Albrecht Dürer German Miniscule Early 16th century.

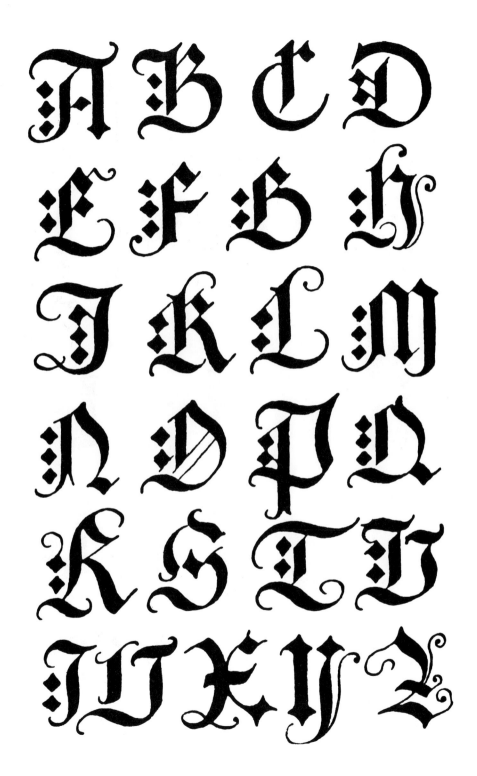

Albrecht Dürer Gothic Capitals Penwork. Early 16th century.

ABCDE
FGHIJK
LMNOP
QRSTU
VWXYZ
abcdefghijklmn
opqrstuvwxyz

Stencilled Alphabet Adapted from E. Grasset and M. P. Verneuil.